# HISTORY OF THE TEMPLE OF THE EMERALD BUDDHA

BY

# PROFESSOR M.C. SUBHADRADIS DISKUL

PUBLISHED BY THE BUREAU OF THE ROYAL HOUSEHOLD

THE PROCEEDS FROM THE SALE FOR THE RESTORATION
OF THE TEMPLE OF THE EMERALD BUDDHA

# FOREWORD

The Temple of the Emerald Buddha is both a sacred structure and the repository of the spirit of the entire Thai people. Not only is it a site where royal ceremonies are performed nearly the whole year round, but it is also a place to which the people repair for many purposes: to listen to sermons on Buddhist holy days and Sundays, to venerate the Emerald Buddha for auspicious benefits, to engage in meditation in order to develop a peaceful mind, to admire the beauty of the temple, or to study for themselves many aspects of art, etc.

Apart from the Thai people, many foreigners also come often to visit the Temple of the Emerald Buddha. Whenever there are important guests, Professor M.C. Subhadradis Diskul is usually called upon to act as guide. He is an expert on this Temple and has more personal association with it than any other individual.

This booklet in your hands will help you understand the history of the Temple of the Emerald Buddha with its various structures erected during different reigns. Through this booklet the pride of the Thai people in their common cultural heritage will be enhanced, and I hope its contents will arouse them to appreciate and safeguard our national heritage for a long time to come.

Sirindhorn

*(H.R.H. Princess Maha Chakri Sirindhorn)*

1.· *Inside the ubosoth of the Temple of the Emerald Buddha. The Emerald Buddha is wearing his rainy season costume.*

3

2. *The face of the Buddha image dedicated to King Rama I.*
3. *The face of the Buddha image dedicated to King Rama II.*

4

4. *Phra Samputtha Panni (at the back) and the Victory Buddha (in Front).*
5. *Mural painting representing the Earth Goddess wringing out waters of merit from her hair. Inside the ubosoth of the Temple of the Emerald Buddha, facing the main image.*

7

6. *Two gilt stupas in fron of the Royal Pantheon.*
7. *Garuda holding a naga. Around the base of the ubosoth of the Temple of the Emerald Buddha*

8. *Bronze image of a half-human and half-deer in front of the Royal Pantheon.*
9. *Demon and monkey caryatides of one of the two gilt stupas.*
10. *Monument dedicated to Kings Rama I, II, and III.*

8

9

11. *Viharn Yod*
12. *Mother-of-pearl inlaid door-panel of the Ayudhya period on the northern side of Viharn Yod.*
13. *Model of Angkor Wat.*

13              12

15

14. *Ho Phra Monthien Tham (the Supplementary Library).*
15. *Belfry.*

16

16. *Figure of a seated hermit.*
17. *Demon gate-guardian.*

*18. Ramakien mural painting on the gallery around the Temple of the Emerald Buddha.*

# The History of the Temple of the Emerald Buddha

by

## Professor M.C. Subhadradis Diskul*

The tradition of constructing a Buddhist temple in the precincts of the Royal Palace has existed in Thailand since the Sukhothai period (1240-c. 1438 A.D.). When King Rama I (1782-1809) of Bangkok established the city of Bangkok, or Ratanakosin, as his capital in 1782 A.D., he had the Temple of the Emerald Buddha constructed in the eastern section of the Royal Palace in order to install the Emerald Buddha, which he had obtained from the city of Vientiane in Laos. The construction took two years to finish and the famous image was transferred from Thonburi to the present site in 1784.

The construction of the Temple of the Emerald Buddha in the First Reign can be divided into two periods. During the first the boundaries of the Temple on the north and the east were even more limiting than at the present time. The temple compound was enclosed by galleries (no. 22 on the plan, at the back), and in the south was built the *ubosoth* (the ordination hall, no.1) enshrining the Emerald Buddha as its main image. Other construction, as we shall see, was to follow.

*The author would like to thank Mrs. Virginia M. di Crocco for improving the English language in this text.

**The History of the Emerald Buddha.** The Emerald Buddha is in reality carved from a large piece of green jade. According to a reliable chronicle, in 1434 A.D. lightning struck a *chedi* in Chiengrai in northern Thailand and a Buddha statue covered with stucco was found inside. The image was brought into the abbot's residence and one day he noticed that the stucco on the nose had flaked off and the image inside was green in colour. He removed all the stucco and found the Emerald Buddha. (The word *emerald* here only means "green coloured" in Thai.)

People then flocked to worship this precious statue. At that time the town of Chiengrai was under the rule of the king of Chiengmai. The latter, King Samfangkaen, sent an elephant to bring the Emerald Buddha to Chiengmai, but each time the elephant arrived at the junction with the road to the city of Lampang, it ran to that town. The king sent an elephant out three times and each time the same incident occurred, so he thought that the spirits guarding the Emerald Buddha wanted to stay in Lampang. Thus the Emerald Buddha was allowed to remain in Lampang for 32 years, until 1468, when Chiengmai had a powerful king, King Tiloka. He had the Emerald Buddha brought to Chiengmai and, according to one chronicle, installed the image in the eastern niche of a large *stupa* called Chedi Luang.

In 1551 the king of Chiengmai, who had no son, died. One of his daughters was married to the king of Laos. She had borne one son, named Prince Chaichettha. When the king of Chiengmai died the ministers of Chiengmai invited the prince, who was fifteen, to become king and he accepted. However, when his father, the king of Laos, passed away, King Chaichettha wanted to go back to his own country, so in 1552 he returned to Luang Prabang, the then capital of Laos, taking the Emerald Buddha with him, and promised the ministers of Chiengmai to come back.

He never returned nor did he send back the Emerald Buddha, so the image remained at Luang Prabang for twelve years.

In 1564 King Chaichettha could not resist the Burmese army of King Bayinnaung; thus he moved his capital down to Vientiane and the Emerald Buddha remained there for 214 years.

In 1778, during the Thonburi period, when King Rama I of Bangkok was still a general, he captured Vientiane and brought the Emerald Buddha back to Thailand. With the establishment of Bangkok as the capital, the Emerald Buddha became the palladium of Thailand and has been ever since. The image was moved from Thonburi to the Temple of the Emerald Buddha in Bangkok on 22 March 1784.

King Rama I had two seasonal costumes made for the Emerald Buddha, one for summer and one for the rainy season. King Rama III (1824-1851) added another one for winter. The ceremony of changing the costumes of the Emerald Buddha takes place three times a year. In the old days the king would spray lustral water only on the princes and officials who were attending the ceremony inside the *ubosoth*. But during the present reign, His Majesty the King also sprays lustral water upon his subjects who are waiting outside the ordination hall. It can be regarded as a new tradition inaugurated in this reign.

The lap of the Emerald Buddha is 48.3 cm. wide and the height, including the base, is 66 cm. The image is in a seated position, with the right leg resting on the left one. Judging from this iconographic factor, one could conclude that it was carved in Northern Thailand not much earlier than the fifteenth century A.D. and belongs to the late Northern Thai, that is to say, the late Chiengsaen or Chiengmai school. If this is so, it must have been made not long before its discovery in the *stupa* in Chiengrai.

On the other hand, the Emerald Buddha, which is in the attitude of meditation, looks much like some of the Buddha images of Southern India and Sri Lanka, especially those in this same attitude. The attitude of meditation has never been popular in Thai images of the Buddha. Thus one might assign the origin of the Emerald Buddha to one of the aforementioned countries.

Inside the *ubosoth* (no. 1) containing the Emerald Buddha there also are other interesting items:

1. The gold-covered wooden throne, made in the First Reign, on which the Emerald Buddha sits. H.R.H. Prince Naris, one of the most famous architects and artists of the Bangkok period, admired it greatly. He wrote that it was the best of its kind he had ever seen in Bangkok. Originally the golden throne rested on what now is its lowest base, but King Rama III added the intermediary one.

2. The mother-of-pearl door-panels made in the First Reign of Bangkok following the style of the late Ayudhya period.

3. Two large standing crowned Buddha images dedicated to King Rama I and King Rama II (1809-1824). In the reign of King Rama III, the public called the reign of King Rama I "The Beginning Reign" and that of King Rama II "The Middle Reign." King Rama III thought that giving each reign such an appellation was a bad omen for the dynasty since it suggested that his would be the last reign. Thus in 1841 he had two large standing crowned Buddha images cast in bronze. About 3 m. high, they are in the attitude of calming the ocean and are covered with gold and precious gems. He named the one placed on the northern side of the Emerald Buddha "Phra Puttha Yodfa Chulalok," and the one on the south, "Phra Puttha Lerdla Napalai," and dedicated them, respectively, to King Rama I and King Rama II. A proclamation was then issued for the public to call the first two kings by these official names.

These two Buddha images were worshipped at the ceremony in which officials took the oath of allegiance to the king beginning with the reign of King Rama IV (King Mongkut, 1851-1868). The ceremony was discontinued, however, after the revolution in 1932 leading to the establishment of the constitutional monarchy.

4. A small bronze Buddha image called Phra Samputtha Panni created by King Rama IV in 1830 when he was still in the monkhood. The monk-prince invented a new type of Buddha image without a cranial protuberance, wearing a pleated monastic robe and seated in the attitude of meditation. Phra Samputtha Panni has been placed in front of the throne supporting the Emerald Buddha.

5. Ten crowned Buddha images in bronze in the attitude of calming the ocean. They are covered with gold and were installed in pairs on the base supporting the throne of the Emerald Buddha. They were created by successive kings of the present Chakri Dynasty and were dedicated to high members of the royal family, both male and female, from the First to the Third Reigns.

6. Mural paintings inside the *ubosoth*. The scene of the Buddhist cosmology (the Three Worlds of Desire, Form and Non-Form) on the western wall behind the Emerald Buddha and that of the Enlightenment of the Buddha on the eastern, or front wall, were painted in the reign of King Rama I. At that time there probably was portrayed on the upper part of the lateral walls the assembly of celestial beings who came to worship the main Buddha image in the *ubosoth,* a feature typical of the late Ayudhya and early Bangkok painting styles. The walls between the windows were decorated with scenes from the Life of the Buddha. King Rama III had the lateral walls repainted. Above the windows on both the north and the south were depicted scenes from the Life of the Buddha whereas between the windows various scenes from the *jataka* (previous lives of the Buddha) were shown. On the

lower part of the northern wall a royal procession on land is depicted and the southern side shows a riverine procession. These paintings still exist.

In the scene of the Enlightenment of the Buddha one always sees the Buddha seated under the Bodhi tree either in the attitude of meditation (having the right hand on the left one in the lap) or subduing Mara (having the right hand on the right knee with the palm facing inward and the fingers pointing to the ground, with the left hand on the lap). The Earth Goddess is underneath, wringing out water from her hair, and the Buddha is flanked on both sides by the army of Mara (evil spirits); on one side they are trying to attack the Master and on the other they have already been subjugated. According to the Life of the Buddha, before his Enlightenment Mara came and asked the Buddha what right he had to attain Enlightenment in this life and bring people out of ignorance. The Buddha replied that in his past lives (a Buddhist believes in rebirth) he had accumulated enough merit to attain Enlightenment in this life. (Usually when one performs deeds of merit, even nowadays, one has to pour water on the ground to make the Earth Goddess one's witness and also to give merit to the dead.) The Buddha then changed his attitude from meditation to that of subduing Mara by placing his right hand on his right knee, calling the Earth Goddess up from the ground. She wrung from her hair the water accumulated from the deeds of merit that the Buddha had performed in his previous lives and this drowned the whole of Mara's army. The Buddha then continued his meditation until he arrived at the Supreme Enlightenment.

Sometimes this scene is explained as an allegory or personification of the thought of the Buddha. During this period the Buddha was undergoing a mental struggle as to whether he should go back to worldly pleasure or continue his meditation until he arrived at the Supreme Enlightenment. Once he had decided to continue his meditation, he put his right hand on his right knee as a sign of his determination not to get up from his seat until his great desire had been accomplished.

7. Bronze lion door-guardians. There are altogether twelve, in six pairs. It had been believed that the pair guarding the main central door of the *ubosoth* on the east, which can be entered only by the Chief of State, was brought from Cambodia by command of King Rama I and the rest were copied in that reign. However, Professor Boisselier, the renowned French expert on Khmer Art, examined the central pair of lion-guardians and concluded that the design on their chest is Thai in style rather than Khmer. They probably were cast by Thai artisans copying Khmer lions. On both sides of the main staircase in front of the Royal Pantheon (no. 9) on the east sit two stone lion-guardians. Though they have been very much restored, one can perceive that they belong to the Khmer Bayon style (about the early thirteenth century A.D.). Therefore it might be that this pair of stone lions was brought from Cambodia during the rign of King Rama I and the bronze ones were cast in that reign to copy them.

In addition to the *ubosoth* containing the Emerald Buddha (no. 1), King Rama I also had twelve small open pavilions built around it (no. 2). North of the *ubosoth* at the site of the present Library or Phra Mondop (no. 11), he had a library in the late Ayudhya and early Bangkok fashions constructed in the middle of a pond in order to keep the termites from coming to eat the holy palm-leaf manuscripts. The building was also used in that reign by those translating foreign correspondence. On the east of the pond, at the present site of the Royal Pantheon (no. 9), two gilded *stupa* were built on the ground in commemoration of the king's parents. A belfry was also constructed south of the *ubosoth* for a bronze bell (no. 4), valued for its rich sound, that been removed from Wat Saket in Bangkok.

In 1788 King Rama I had the Tripitaka (the Buddhist Holy Manuscripts) revised at Wat Mahathat, and after the revision was completed, transferred a new copy of it to the new library inside the Temple of the Emerald Buddha and ordered a grand celebration. Unfortunately sparks from fireworks fell on the roof of the library and burnt it down but the Tripitaka was saved in time.

During the second phase of construction under King Rama I, the king had the pond under the library filled up, enlarged the boundaries of the Temple on both its eastern and northern sides to the present limits and constructed many other buildings.

On top of the pond that had been filled up the king had a new library (no. 11) built, containing a large, beautiful mother-of-pearl inlaid book-cabinet to house the Tripitaka. This superb book-cabinet was made under the supervision of Chao Praya Mahasena, the founder of the Bunnag family. H.R.H. Prince Naris admired this new library very much for its style and decorations, such as a bronze snake with human faces, rather than reptilian ones on the railing of each staircase, the demon door-guardians and the mother-of-pearl inlaid door-panels.

On the enlarged grounds to the north, the king's younger brother, the Prince of the Palace to the Front, built for his brother a supplementary library, Ho Phra Monthien Tham (no. 18), housing the rest of the Tripitaka. It was also used as a site for the translation of foreign correspondence. Inside are kept many beautiful mother-of-pearl inlaid book-cabinets, and the door of the building, which is decorated with the same material, dates back to 1752 in the late Ayudhya period, during the reign of King Boromkot (1732-1758). The mural paintings inside, which originally dated from the early Bangkok period, have recently been totally restored.

On the west and next to the Supplementary Library near the present Viharn Yod (no. 19) was built the White Viharn for the keeping of Buddha images and the Viharn Phra Thep Bidorn. Phra Thep Bidorn was probably a Hindu image and was believed to represent King U Thong, the founder of Ayudhya, the capital prior to Bangkok. King Rama I had had the sculpture brought down to Bangkok and recast into a crowned Buddha image covered with silver.

Next to the Viharn Phra Thep Bidorn on the west another *viharn* (congregation hall) was constructed to house a large standing Buddha image of copper alloy. It is 4 m. high and is called Phra Nak. This image had been moved down from Ayudhya and the building containing it was named Ho Phra Nak (no. 20).

In front of the Temple of the Emerald Buddha on the east, the king had eight *prang* (towers) constructed (no. 21). They were dedicated respectively from the north to the south to the following important elements of Buddhism: the Buddha, the Dhamma (the Law), the Sangha (Buddhist monks), the Bhikshuni (Buddhist nuns who existed in the old days), Pacchekabodhi Buddhas (Buddhas who attained Enlightenment but never preached), the *chakravarti* (great emperors), the Bodhisattva (the Buddha in his previous lives, according to Theravada Buddhism) and the Maitreya (the future Buddha).

In the reign of King Rama II nothing was added, but in the reign of his son, King Rama III, the whole temple was restored since many buildings had decayed and were in need of repair to make them appropriate for the celebration of the fiftieth anniversary of Bangkok in 1832. He began the restoration in 1831, one year before the festivities.

The king had the superstructure of the *ubosoth* restored and changed the decoration on its exterior walls from gold on red lacquer to gilt-stucco decorated with coloured glass, which is as it appears today. He also had 112 figures of *garuda* (the king of birds) holding *naga* (the king of snakes) cast in bronze to ornament the base. The mural paintings inside were newly painted as mentioned above except for the scenes of the Buddhist cosmology and the Enlightenment of the Buddha, respectively, on the western and eastern walls. The golden throne of the Emerald Buddha was heightened, as noted previously, by an intermediary base. The king had the superstructure of the galleries around the temple changed and the whole story of the *Ramakien* (the Thai version of the Hindu epic, the *Ramayana*) repainted. The White Viharn of King Rama I was demolished, and the Viharn Yod (no. 19), with its superstructure in the form of a Thai crown ornamented with multi-coloured pieces of glazed terracotta, was built in its place. The mother-of-pearl inlaid door of this structure dates back to 1753 in the reign of King Boromkot of the late Ayudhya period.

H.R.H. Prince Damrong Rajanubhab, father of Thai history and archaeology, surmised that originally the area at the northern side of the Temple of the Emerald Buddha contained four buildings, respectively, from the east to the west: the Supplementary Library (Ho Phra Monthien Tham, no. 18), the White Viharn, the Ho Phra Thep Bidorn and the Ho Phra Nak. But in the reign of King Rama III the need arose for a rather large building in which to keep the ashes of the deceased members of the present Chakri Dynasty, so the king had the Ho Phra Thep Bidorn and the original Ho Phra Nak pulled down, and built instead a large building (no. 20) to preserve the ashes of the deceased princes and princesses. The images of Phra Thep Bidorn (the crowned Buddha image clad in silver) and Phra Nak (the large standing Buddha image in copper alloy) were transferred to the Viharn Yod (no. 19) and have remained there ever since.

The large new building, though containing only the ashes of the deceased members of the present dynasty, has continued, however, to be called Ho Phra Nak (no. 20) up to the present day.

Apart from the above-mentioned buildings, King Rama III restored structures such as the Library (Phra Mondop), the Supplementary Library (Ho Phra Monthien Tham), the small open pavilions around the *ubosoth,* the belfry, the two golden *stupa* and the eight *prang* (towers), etc. He embellished the grounds by constructing small artificial stone hills, stone seats, and flower pots, and lined the paths and entrances with Chinese stone sculptures. The king also had a figure of a seated hermit, who was supposed to be a great physician, cast in bronze and installed behind the *ubosoth* to the west in front of a gate (no. 8). A grinding stone and a mortar were placed before the figure so that people could come to worship and grind their medicine for greater efficacy.

In the reign of King Rama IV (King Mongkut, 1851-1868), much reconstruction took place. The tall terrace on which the Library (Phra Mondop, no. 11) stands was enlarged both on its western and eastern sides and two tiers of stone railings were built around it. Six gates and staircases leading up to the Library were added as well as galleries on the east and the west. On the east a gate with a superstructure in the form of a Thai crown was built, flanked by two pavilions. On the west a gate with a four-sided top and a pavilion were constructed.

In front of the Library (no. 11) on the east the king built a pavilion with a *prang* (tower) summit, which is now called the Royal Pantheon (no. 9). It was begun in 1856. At first the king wanted to transfer the Emerald Buddha there as he thought it was improper for the Buddha to be lower than the Tripitaka (the Law). But after the building was finished, it was found to be too small to perform any ceremony inside, so it was left vacant. The two gilt redented *stupa* (no. 10) also on the terrace in front of the Royal Pantheon on the east might have been built in this reign to replace the former two constructed by King Rama I, which would have been on the ground.

To the west of the Library (Phra Mondop, no. 11) a *stupa* was constructed in imitation of a large one at Wat Phra Si Sanpet at Ayudhya (no. 12). The construction began in 1855. The *stupa* was called Phra Si Ratana Chedi and relics of the Buddha were enshrined in it. The golden mosaic adorning it at present, however, was not added until the reign of King Mongkut's son, King Rama V (King Chulalongkorn, 1868-1910).

The wooden superstructure of the Library (no. 11) was restored, and the thin flat pieces of silver which paved the floor inside were replaced by silver mats.

To the north of the Library King Mongkut had built a model of Angkor Wat (no. 13) as it was during the period when Cambodia was still a vassal state of Thailand. This model was finished in the reign of King Rama V for the centenary celebration of Bangkok.

At the southeastern corner of the *ubosoth,* a *viharn* with a *prang* superstructure was built to house an old *chedi* brought down from northern Thailand, and in front of this *viharn* was constructed a building to enshrine a bronze Buddha image called the Gandhara Buddha. The image had been cast in the First Reign of Bangkok for the ceremony of asking for rain during the agricultural season (no. 3). This Buddha has a halo in the form of a lotus bud or a gem. He wears a monastic robe in a Chinese fashion and his right hand is in the attitude of calling down the rain whereas his left hand is trying to catch it. These two buildings were ornamented with the present terracotta glazed tiles in the reign of King Rama V. King Rama IV also had a site prepared in front of the *viharn* enshrining the Gandhara Buddha for the stone seat of King Ram Khamhaeng the Great (1279-1299) which King Rama IV, when still in the monkhood, had brought down from the town of Sukhothai. (This stone seat has now been removed to another site.)

To the south of the *ubosoth* a new belfry was constructed, probably on the site of the original one (no. 4).

Behind the *ubosoth* on the west, King Rama IV also had constructed a pavilion having a *prang* superstructure decorated with glazed teracotta; this was to house an old bronze *prang* called Phra Pothithat Piman (no. 6). He then had a small structure built on either side of this central pavilion. The northern structure, named Ho Rachakaramanusorn (no. 7), houses thirty-four small bronze Buddha images in various attitudes dedicated to the thirty-three kings of Ayudhya and one king of Thonburi. These small Buddha images in various attitudes had been cast by command of King Rama III from copper found at Chantuk in the province of Nakhon Ratchasima (Khorat) in northeastern Thailand. The king had asked his uncle, H.R.H. Prince Paramanuchit, who was in the monkhood, to invent forty attitudes for Buddha images after the life story of the Master, but he had only thirty-four images cast. The mural paintings inside the building depicting the history of the Ayudhya period were executed by Khrua In Khong, an eminent painter who was the first Thai to use western perspective. Inside the southern building called Ho Rachapongsanusorn (no. 5), which was dedicated to the kings of the Chakri Dynasty, are now installed eight small Buddha images in different attitudes, each one protected by a many-tiered umbrella. The mural paintings inside portray the life of King Rama I or the history of Bangkok and probably were painted by an artist other than Khrua In Khong as the workmanship is not all the same.

King Rama IV also had both the roof of the *ubosoth* and the mural paintings on the lateral walls restored after the original style. The floor of the *ubosoth* was renovated and the windows were changed totally into mother-of-pearl inlaid work. The Chinese door-guardians and the angel window-guardians which had originally been painted were changed to gilt-stucco work decorated with coloured glass. The glazed terracotta tiles around the base of the *ubosoth* were replaced.

The king also began the restoration of the galleries and the repainting of story of the *Ramakien;* this work was finished in the reign of King Rama V.

In the reign of King Rama V Bangkok was to celebrate its centenary anniversary in 1882; therefore, in 1880 the king asked all his younger brothers, some other princes and various officials to help him with the total renovation of the Temple of the Emerald Buddha. During this period, apart from the restoration of the already existing architecture, the gilt bronze figures of mythical beings presently on the terrace around the Royal Pantheon (no. 9) were cast and the Phra Si Ratana Chedi (no. 12) was entirely covered with golden mosaic. A number of stucco trays with conical covers supposedly containing betel nut sets were added as decoration on a lower stone railing around the terrace in the central part of the temple. Marble slabs engraved with poems describing the *Ramakien* story were embedded in gallery pillars opposite paintings of the same episode, whereas poems concerning the incarnations of Vishnu and the origins of demon and monkey families were placed on the walls near the paintings. These poems were composed by the king, some princes, officials and Buddhist monks who were well versed in poetry. Demon and monkey caryatides were added to support the two gilt *stupa* (no. 10) in front of the Royal Pantheon. Many stone items to decorate the temple were also ordered. Two large pairs of demon-guardians at the gates were probably added during this period in imitation of the other eight demon gate-guardians made in the Third Reign.

The king also had monuments erected for his ancestors and himself on the terrace of the Royal Pantheon. The one at the northwestern corner (no. 14) was dedicated to Kings Rama I, Rama II and Rama III, designated by their respective emblems, the upper part of a crown, a *garuda* holding a *naga,* and a pavilion. These gilt-bronze emblems were placed inside a throne which was put on top of a marble square pillar. Models in bronze of the white and other important elephants of each reign surround its base. At the southwestern corner (no. 15) a second monument was dedicated to King Rama IV and bears his emblem, a crown, inside a throne. The third one, which was for himself, has his own emblem, a small crown (Chulalongkorn) placed on a cushion, inside a throne, and was erected at the southwestern corner of the Royal Pantheon (no. 16). The second and third monuments were also surrounded at the base with models in bronze of the white and other important elephants of each reign.

As for the foreign objects that King Rama V had acquired from various countries, he arranged them in the Temple of the Emerald Buddha; for instance, the five volcanic stone Dhyani Buddhas of the 8th century A.D. that the king had obtained from Borobudur on the island of Java. He had them placed on the terrace south of the Library (Phra Mondop, no. 11), but in the reign of King Rama VI (King Vajiravudh, 1910-1925), the king removed four of them and enshrined them in the niches of a new *chedi* that he had erected at Wat Rachathiwat in Bangkok. The fifth one was transferred to Wat Bovornniwet, also in Bangkok. As for the four stone Dhyani Buddhas that King Rama V obtained from Chandi Plaosan (9th-10th century A.D.), also on Java, the King had them placed at the four corners of the Library (Phra Mondop, no.11). But for the Bicentenary Celebration of Bangkok in 1982, H.R.H. Princess Maha Chakri Sirindhorn, the second daughter of the present king (H.M. King Bhumibol, Rama IX), as Chairman of the Committee for the Restoration of the Temple of the Emerald Buddha for that auspicious occasion, had them transferred for their protection and preservation to the Museum of the Temple of the Emerald Buddha which she created inside the old building of the Department of Pages on the northern side of the Dusit Mansion in the Grand Palace. She had copies put at their previous sites, and also removed to the new museum four pairs of stone statues portraying characters in dramas composed by King Rama II: the *Ramakien, Kraitong, Sangtong* or *The Prince of the Golden Conch,* and *Manora.* These statues were probably carved in the reign of King Rama III and placed at the four corners of the *ubosoth* at that time.

Foreign objects dating back to the reign of King Rama V and the later period which are still kept inside the *ubosoth* include a pulpit, flower pots and decorative figures of Italian marble which might have been offered by King Rama V to the Emerald Buddha after one of his two trips to Europe, and gifts brought by others.

The total restoration of the Temple of the Emerald Buddha by King Rama V in 1882 might be considered as the second largest restoration since the temple was built.

One evening in 1903 a great fire broke out on the roof of the Royal Pantheon (no. 9) because the electrical wires were worn. As a result its superstructure had to be rebuilt and later on the wooden roof of the Library (Phra Mondop, no 11) was also restored. This restoration was accomplished in the reign of King Rama VI.

In the reign of King Rama VI the king had the Royal Pantheon, which had been empty since the time of its founder, King Rama IV, turned into the Royal Pantheon of the Chakri Dynasty. Five statues of the past kings were removed in 1918 to the Royal Pantheon from the Sivalai Mansion, which is inside the Grand Palace to the south of the temple. At this time the two gilt *stupa* (no. 10) were also moved to their present sites east of the terrace. Four grand marble staircases were constructed leading up to the top part of the terrace on the east, the north and the south as well as leading up to the Phra Si Ratana Chedi (no. 12) on the southern side. The steps of the six staircases of the *ubosoth* (no. 1) were lowered in order to facilitate climbing them and were paved with marble. The stone seat of King Ram Khamhaeng the Great, which had originally been set up in front of the *viharn* of the Gandhara Buddha (no. 3), was transported to the Dusit Pavilion and installed there as a throne underneath a white nine-tiered umbrella, one of the royal regalia.

In the reign of King Rama VII (King Prajadhipok, 1925-1934), Bangkok celebrated its 150th anniversary in 1932 and the Temple of the Emerald Buddha was totally restored again, especially the paintings of the *Ramakien* along the galleries (no. 22), which had been much damaged by rain and dampness. They were completely repainted. The stone seat of King Ram Khamhaeng the Great, which had been transformed into a throne in the Dusit Mansion, was transferred by command of the king to the Ananta Samakhom Audience Hall, but after the *coup d'état* in June 1932 changing the system of absolute monarchy into a constitutional one, the king ordered that the stone seat be taken back to the Viharn Yod in the Temple of the Emerald Buddha (no. 19) and preserved there without the white nine-tiered umbrella.

During the present reign, that of King Bhumibol or King Rama IX, Bangkok celebrated its bicentenary in 1982. H.R.H.

Princess Maha Chakri Sirindhorn, as Chairman of the Committee for the Restoration of the Temple of the Emerald Buddha, received a tremendous amount of financial aid from the public apart from the budget set by the government. Every building in the temple was restored in detail as well as the golden throne of the Emerald Buddha, the Buddha images in the *ubosoth* and the paintings of the *Ramakien* along the galleries. The stone seat from the Sukhothai period was removed from the Viharn Yod to be installed as a throne under a white nine-tiered umbrella in the new museum so that the public can pay respect to and remember the beneficence of King Ram Khamhaeng the Great. Also in this museum are displayed the seasonal costumes of the Emerald Buddha, various offerings presented to that sacred image, and some samples of architectural fragments that have been replaced by new ones. The Princess also had a monument erected on the northwestern corner of the Royal Pantheon (no. 17) in commemoration of the bicentenary of Bangkok. It consists of the four emblems of Kings Rama VI, VII, VIII and IX, respectively: the weapon of Indra that causes lightning *(vajiravudh),* the emblem of three arrows under a crown, a male divinity, and the number 9 inside a discus with a nine-tiered umbrella on top. These four gilt-bronze emblems were set inside a throne which was placed upon a square marble pillar surrounded at its base with bronze models of the white and other important elephants of their respective reigns. This monument resembles the three others dedicated to their ancestors (nos. 14, 15 and 16) which were erected during the centenary celebration of Bangkok.

It can be concluded that the Temple of the Emerald Buddha, the most sacred temple of Thailand, has been restored in every alternate reign. It was constructed in the reign of King Rama I and largely restored in the reigns of Kings Rama III, V, VII and IX. In other words, it has had major repairs every fifty years.

# Plan of the Temple of the Emerald Buddha

1.  The *ubosoth* containing the Emerald Buddha.
2.  Twelve small open pavilions.
3.  Viharn of the Gandhara Buddha image.
4.  Belfry.
5.  Ho Rachapongsanusorn.
6.  Phra Pothithat Piman.
7.  Ho Rachakaramanusorn.
8.  Figure of a seated hermit.
9.  The Royal Pantheon.
10. Two gilt *stupa*.
11. Phra Mondop (the Library).
12. Phra Si Ratana Chedi.
13. Model of Angkor Wat.
14. Monument of Kings Rama I, II and III.
15. Monument of King Rama IV (King Mongkut).
16. Monument of King Rama V (King Chulalongkorn).
17. Monument of Kings Rama VI, VII. VIII and IX.
18. Ho Phra Monthien Tham (the Supplementary Library).
19. Viharn Yod.
20. Viharn Phra Nak.
21. Eight *prang* (towers).
22. Galleries.

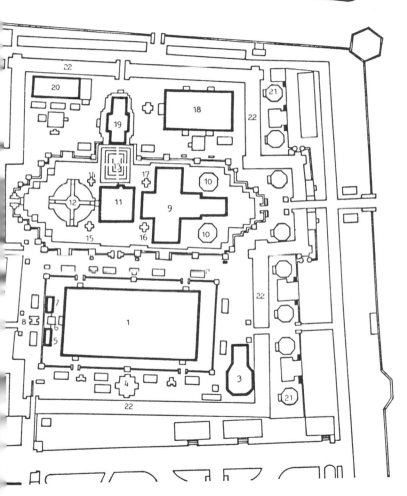

# GLOSSARY

**Angkor Wat** The most famous Khmer monument in Cambodia built by King Suryavarman II in the first half of the 12th century A.D. and dedicated to Vishnu.

**Ayudhya** The capital of Siam or Thailand from 1350 to 1767 A.D., ruled by 33 (sometimes reckoned as 34) kings.

**Bangkok** or Ratanakosin, the capital of Thailand since 1782.

**Bayon** The name of a Khmer temple built by King Jayavarman VII in the centre of the town of Angkor Thom. It is also used as the name of a Khmer school of art during the late 12th to the early 13th century A.D.

**Bodhisattva** Saints in Mahayana Buddhism who are the saviours of the Mahayanists. In Theravada Buddhism this name means the future Buddha, usually in his previous incarnations.

**Buddha** The Enlightened One. In Mahayana Buddhism there are many levels of Buddhahood but in Theravada Buddhism there is only one historical Buddha, Srisakyamuni or Gautama.

**Buddhist cosmology** The three worlds of Buddhism : *kamadhatu* (the world of desire), *rupadhatu* (the world of form) and the *arupadhatu* (the world of non-existence). In art, usually the first two stages are represented by hell, earth and heaven.

**candi** or **chandi** A word usually preceding the name of a monument in Indonesia. According to some scholars this word has the same meaning as *chedi*. According to others, however, it derives from the word *Caṇḍi,* the goddess of death, another name of Uma, the

39

consort of Siva, one of the greatest Hindu gods; the monument is so called because it is believed to contain the ashes of the dead. This latter theory is still being argued.

**Chakri** The name of the present dynasty of Thailand, represented by an emblem consisting of a discus *(chakra)* and a three-pronged weapon *(tri)*.

**chedi** From Sanskrit **caitya** or Pali **cetiya**, meaning an object of worship. In Thailand it is used to signify a solid monument built to enshrine the relics of the Buddha or those of his disciples and also to contain the ashes of the dead. The same meaning as **stupa**.

**Chiengmai** The name of the largest town in northern Thailand. It was founded by King Mangrai in 1297 and was the capital of the Thai kingdom of Lanna Thai until the middle of the 16th century A.D. when it was captured by the Burmese. Since then it was sometimes independent and sometimes a vassal state of Ayudhya or Burma until it was definitely incorporated into the present-day Thailand in the latter part of the 18th century.

**garuda** The king of birds and mount of Vishnu, one of the greatest Hindu gods. The motif of a *garuda* holding a *naga* (the king of serpents) is believed to have the power to chase away evil spirits.

**Hinduism** A religion in India that developed from Brahmanism. In Hinduism, there are three chief gods *(Trimurti)* : Brahma (the creator), Siva (the destroyer) and Vishnu (the preserver). In Hinduism to destroy is also to create, as Hindus believe in rebirth.

**Indra** Originally the chief god of war and thunder during the Vedic period. In Hinduism and Buddhism he is the chief god of the Tavatimsa Heaven (the heaven of the thirty-three gods) on top of the Sumeru mountain. His weapon is a thunderbolt *(vajiravudh)* and his mount is the three-headed elephant, Airavata or Erawan. His complexion is green.

**jataka** Previous lives of the Buddha, usually 550 in number, but the most important are the last ten.

**Khmer** An ancient race in Cambodia, the ancestors of the present-day Cambodians. They created the ancient Khmer empire.

**Mahayana Buddhism** "Greater Vehicle" or "Greater Means of Progression", a form of Buddhism that incorporates many aspects of Brahmanism (ancient Hinduism). In Mahayana Buddhism there are many Buddhas and Bodhisattvas. It is supposed to have begun in northern India in about the 1st century A.D. In late Mahayana Buddhism there are the Adi Buddha, who is the creator of the World, and the five Dhyani Buddhas, with one in the centre and the others at each of the cardinal directions. There are many Bodhisattvas as well.

**Maitreya** The Bodhisattva who will be reborn as the future Buddha, according to both Theravada and Mahayana Buddhism.

**mandapa** or **mondop** (in Thai) A square structure with a pyramidal pointed roof.

**naga** King of serpents, enemy of *garuda* (king of birds).

**prang** A structure in Thailand in imitation of a Khmer tower.

**Ramakien** The Thai version of the Hindu epic, the *Ramayana*. There are many Thai versions of the *Ramakien* but the one depicted along the galleries of the Temple of the Emerald Buddha follows the version of King Rama I. The story develops like that of Helen of Troy. The heroine of the story, Sita, is abducted by a great demon, Ravana, and her husband, Rama, follows with an army of monkeys. Many battles ensue until Rama regains his wife upon the defeat of the demons.

The beginning point of the paintings along the galleries is on the north, at the eastern side of the gate facing Viharn Yod (no. 19); the story then proceeds to the east. Those who are interested should buy the album entitled **The Ramakien Mural Paintings along the Galleries of the Temple of the Emerald Buddha** (฿ 1,200 per copy) from the Treasury Section of the Bureau of the Royal Household during official hours.

**stupa** A solid monument originally built to enshrine the relics of the Buddha or of his disciples, or to mark an important site in Buddhism. It evolves from a burial mound with a seat and an umbrella on top. It now has the same meaning as the word *cheḍi* in Thai (see **chedi**).

**Sukhothai** A town that was the capital of an ancient Thai kingdom of the same name in northern Thailand from about the middle of the thirteenth century A.D. to that of the fifteenth. There were nine ruling kings, of whom King Ram Khamhaeng the Great (1279-1299) was the third and the most famous.

**Theravada Buddhism** The "Doctrine of the Elders", representing the traditional Pali heritage of early Buddhism; the Pali Canon is considered by the Theravada sects to be the authentic doctrine. Sometimes it is called Hinayana (Small Vehicle), which is a pejorative name used by the Mahayanists (see **Mahayana Buddhism**).

**Thonburi** A town opposite Bangkok on the other side of the Chao Phraya River. It was the capital of Thailand from 1767 to 1782 A.D., where only one king ruled.

**ubosoth** An edifice inside a Buddhist monastery, surrounded by eight sacred boundary stones and within which the ordination of monks and other rituals can be performed.

**vihara** or **viharn** (in Thai) An edifice inside a Buddhist monastery, enshrining an image or images of the Buddha and where merit-making ceremonies are performed. Originally this word was used for the residence of Buddhist monks.